D1709653

Arctic Foxes

By Maeve T. Sisk

Gareth Stevens
Publishing

Please visit our Web site, www.garethstevens.com. For a free color catalog of all our high-quality books, call toll free 1-800-542-2595 or fax 1-877-542-2596.

Library of Congress Cataloging-in-Publication Data

Sisk, Maeve T.
 Arctic foxes / Maeve T. Sisk.
     p. cm. – (Animals that live in the tundra)
 Includes index.
 ISBN 978-1-4339-3888-7 (pbk.)
 ISBN 978-1-4339-3889-4 (6-pack)
 ISBN 978-1-4339-3887-0 (library binding)
 1. Foxes–Arctic regions–Juvenile literature. I. Title.
 QL737.C22S594 2010
 599.776'4–dc22
                                            2010005916

First Edition

Published in 2011 by
Gareth Stevens Publishing
111 East 14th Street, Suite 349
New York, NY 10003

Designer: Michael J. Flynn
Editor: Therese Shea

Photo credits: Cover, pp. 1, 5, 7, 9, 11, 13, 15, 21, back cover Shutterstock.com; p. 17 Ronald Wittek/Photographers Choice/Getty Images; p. 19 Jeff Foott/ Discovery Channel Images/Getty Images.

Printed in the United States of America

CPSIA compliance information: Batch #CS10GS: For further information contact Gareth Stevens, New York, New York at 1-800-542-2595.

Table of Contents

Hiding in Plain Sight 4

Keeping Out the Cold 10

Finding Food. 16

Family Time 20

Glossary 22

For More Information 23

Index 24

Boldface words appear in the glossary.

Hiding in Plain Sight

Arctic foxes live around the Arctic Ocean. They have a great way to hide. Their coats make them hard to see in the **tundra**.

Arctic foxes have several **layers** of fur. In winter, many arctic foxes have a white outer layer. Others have a blue-gray coat. Both colors blend in with snow.

winter coat

In the spring, arctic foxes **shed** their outer layers. They become gray or brown. These colors blend in with tundra rocks and plants. When it gets colder, the foxes grow winter fur again.

summer coat

Keeping Out the Cold

Arctic foxes have small ears and short noses. Small body parts help keep body heat in. Arctic foxes also have fur on the bottoms of their paws.

small ears

short nose

11

Arctic foxes live in **burrows** under the ground. They can also dig deep into the snow to escape cold tundra winds.

burrow

An arctic fox has a special tail called a "brush." The brush is very thick. The arctic fox wraps itself in its brush to keep warm.

brush

Finding Food

Arctic foxes eat **lemmings**, birds, fish, and other animals. They also eat some plants and berries. Arctic foxes store food for the winter.

Arctic foxes may follow polar bears to get food. After a polar bear kills an animal, the arctic fox eats any leftover meat.

arctic fox

polar bear

Family Time

Arctic foxes **mate** in the spring. Mother arctic foxes may have up to 14 pups! The mother, father, and pups live together for just a few months.

Fast Facts

Height	up to 12 inches (30 centimeters) at the shoulder
Length	up to 27 inches (69 centimeters) from head to rear; tail is up to 14 inches (36 centimeters)
Weight	up to 17 pounds (8 kilograms)
Diet	some plants; animals, such as lemmings, birds, and fish; also, dead animals
Average life span	up to 6 years in the wild

Glossary

burrow: a hole or tunnel dug by an animal as a living space

layer: a thickness that lies over, under, or between other thicknesses

lemming: an animal with a small, thick, furry body that lives in northern areas

mate: to come together to make a baby

shed: to lose fur or hair

tundra: flat, treeless plain with ground that is always frozen

For More Information

Books

Person, Stephen. *Arctic Fox: Very Cool!* New York, NY: Bearport Publishing, 2009.

Stuhr, Carri. *Arctic Foxes.* Minneapolis, MN: Lerner Publications Company, 2009.

Web Sites

Arctic Foxes

animals.nationalgeographic.com/animals/mammals/arctic-fox.html

See a map showing where arctic foxes live as well as many photos of Arctic wildlife.

Arctic Wildlife: Arctic Foxes

www.mnh.si.edu/arctic/html/arctic_fox.html

Read about the arctic fox and other animals of the tundra, including birds and water animals.

Index

Arctic Ocean 4

berries 16

birds 16, 21

brush 14, 15

burrows 12, 13

coats 4, 6, 7, 9

fish 16, 21

fur 6, 8, 10

layers 6, 8

lemmings 16, 21

life span 21

mate 20

paws 10

plants 16, 21

polar bears 18, 19

pups 20

shed 8

short noses 10, 11

small ears 10, 11

tundra 4, 8, 12

About the Author

Maeve T. Sisk is a writer and editor of several children's books. Her love of nature has led to a life of research and study of all things animal. An aspiring Arctic explorer, Maeve lives in New York City, where she often visits the arctic foxes at the zoo.

ML   4/12